A special thanks to Jeanie Calci and Ana Cantu for their help and support in the writing of this book. This book is dedicated to all women of the world and if it solves one argument or life, its purpose has been served.

Inherent in a woman's need to connect with a significant other many a woman has found herself hurt in the process of trying to connect. Women make this journey along the path of life wondering about her relationship with others. If she keeps her focus on her own happiness on this path, a good dog will catch up with her.

To my mother, with the greatest of love and respect for all the many things you have taught me.

Ana Cantu, a self-taught artist who lives in Myrtle Beach, South Carolina.

I0085810

Index:

A book about the complexity of relationships between men and women; which sometimes sounds more like a fight between dogs and cats.

Prologue

Recently, my friend Alicia complained "Julia, I just don't understand men! Here I am, a very attractive woman who never denies my man sex, but he runs off with another woman from England! I never denied him anything and this is how he repays me?"

I said "Come on, Alicia, there are many women who just don't know how to deal with their men. Maybe you were not looking at the situation correctly" I said. She looked at me with a very puzzled look on her face and asked "What do you mean?"

"Well think of it like this" I said "You have this dog and you're trying to train him. So you try to get him to "roll over" and you give him a treat even though he doesn't roll over. Do you think it is going to be easier to get that dog to roll over the next time you try?" I said.

"Let's say you throw the ball and tell your dog to go and fetch. The dog doesn't go fetch. So you give him another treat. Do you think that you are training him to be an obedient, loyal dog if you give him treats even when he does not do what you want him to? NO! You must think of this as if you are training a dog. When you forget that he is nothing but a dog, don't wonder why you are having problems! All men are dogs! So there is really only one question you need to ask yourself. . . "Is he a trainable dog or an un-trainable dog? What you have to remember is he is still a dog!"

Our conversation inspired this book. My friend asked questions and I answered them, sometimes with wisdom, and sometimes with a little sarcasm and humor.

.

Chapter One

"Dogs Are Simple"

"Can you make it easier for women to understand how men think?" Alicia asked.

"In trying to explain the difference between men and women, I thought about a light switch and electricity. There is nothing more complicated than "electricity". It fuels the very essence of the world around us and brings simple enjoyment into every day of our lives. A day without electricity helps us to appreciate how essential it is."

"Women are like electricity. We are complicated and essential to the world's daily survival. Yet, who can truly understand their complexity? Men are more like the "light switch". They serve a very basic purpose. They are at their best when "turned on" and prefer to be that way most of the time. The role of the "light switch" is very basic and yet, if you ask the "light switch" it would think it's more important than it really is. It thinks it can control all the electricity that flows into the world. It over exaggerates its own importance."

"A "light switch" never tries to understand electricity, its source or its complexity. It does not know why it's there or why it suddenly shuts off and on. "Electricity" tries to understand the light switch, often thinking that it must be as complex as electricity. Electricity does not seem to realize how truly simple the switch is."

"The greatest fear of the light switch, or man, but today let's just call them all dogs, are the moment when the electricity wants to "talk" about their relationship. It is at this moment that the switch is faced with its own inadequacy and has been known to panic and suddenly turn off, until it is needed again."

"Electricity rarely realizes that the scariest words to the switch/dogs are "We need to talk". With these words he knows he is heading for trouble and that it's not going to be good. The scariest words to a man are "We need to talk.""

"Women don't realize that dogs are afraid to have those types of talks. Dogs are very basic. They want sex with a beautiful woman who will do what he wants and make sure his life runs well. Women are much better at getting the kids off to school, paying the bills, making sure dinner is on the table and the clothes are cleaned...etc."

"He thinks of her as someone who is there to make his life run smoother, his organizer or handler. Dogs recognize that women have the unique ability to make the day to day aspects of life flow smoother. Magically meals get cooked, laundry gets done and all the right things happen to show up in his suitcase while they are on vacation. Dogs love a woman who takes care of him and makes his life easier."

"Dogs try to figure out how to obtain women. They understand that there are many things they need to do in order to get a woman. They understand they need to take them out on dates and let them know they care about them. Dogs know that courtship includes social activities like movies, dining out, cocktails and interacting with other couples. Dating will require clean underwear, nice cologne and lots of time and attention because these are things women expect and like."

"Most dogs know that women desire dogs, especially at a young age. Countless innocent, women have been deeply hurt by dogs that used them for sex while never really caring about them. Women tend to live their lives for their dogs when they are in their teens and early twenties. A woman's thirties are more for their children. When women reach their forties they start focusing more on themselves and their own needs and desires."

"Women complain about men and we would have to read book after book just to try to understand them. You say they are more like creatures walking on four legs and looking to breed with the first female pooch that comes along." Alicia considered this.

"No. what I am saying is that the dogs just want to copulate with as many pooches as will allow him."

"So how does a woman really understand a man?" Alicia asked.

"You can think of dogs as having their own puzzle. Some have puzzles with thousands of pieces that make up a complex picture. Others have very few pieces to a simple puzzle. But each dog has a puzzle, which is an image of his own life - his self-image. These pieces in total might symbolize his car, his house, his wife, his children, his job or his hobbies of golf, tennis, fishing...etc. The issue for a woman is to figure out what picture the dog's puzzle forms, if she fits into it and how important her position is. A woman has to ask herself, "Am I a big piece of the puzzle or a small piece of the puzzle?"

"To some dogs, the most important part of their puzzle might be their job. They find their self-identity in their jobs. With others, the most important piece might be their charitable work or hunting or fishing. Each of these pieces can be looked upon as being small or large depending on how much time and effort is put into them. Then a woman gets an idea of how big of a piece of the puzzle she is in the man's life. She starts to figure out if she is a big piece of his life or a small piece of his life based on all the things he has in his life that represent his puzzle of his life."

"There are some men, who go to the other extreme and put too much focus on women being different pieces of the puzzle. A man might not have a job, or house or car but he is good looking and does well with the women. So he adds girlfriend after girlfriend to his puzzle. He could have a wife and still want girlfriend after girlfriend. Their ego is fed by being handsome and being able to add conquest after conquest of women to their puzzle."

"These men never seem satisfied with just one woman. This man's self-image/puzzle picture is a Casanova. His primary objective is about gathering as many small puzzle pieces, each one containing a woman. Each woman he has sex with, becomes a piece of his puzzle. His self-image is not good, when he has no job, no family or fun hobby. His own self esteem becomes the driving force for him to obtain pieces to his puzzle. He often aims for what will make him feel better - what will make him feel more positive. He picks up a puzzle piece, in the form of a woman, and feels that he has some special rights to her. It's like purchasing a square on a Monopoly board. Men often measure their importance by how successful they are at attracting and seducing women. Most men think of a woman and sex in terms of a conquest, like an obtaining a car, a house, a job. This is why they let other guys know who they have slept with and who they want to have sex with. It feeds their ego. The most important thing a woman needs to remember is that "SEX" is an ACT of Possessing for a man."

"So you're saying I am just one piece of a man's puzzle?" Alicia was amazed at the logic.

"Yes, in a way, I am saying that. However, the real question is not are you a piece of a puzzle, but rather how large a piece of the puzzle you are. Are you one large piece of the puzzle or are you just one of a thousand small pieces. I really encourage women to set down and with a piece of paper. Then make a puzzle of her man's life. Put all the items that are important to him and put them in portions of how she sees the importance of each piece. This gives her a better idea of how important she really is in his life."

"So I want to be the most important piece of his puzzle." Alicia asked.

"Well that can be dangerous too. If your man has no balance and you are the only piece of this puzzle it can really cause problems in the relationship and women can feel stifled. Or even worse, it can become obsessive and even dangerous."

"It can actually be scary for women when a dog makes her the only piece of his puzzle. These are the dogs that women call stalkers and crazy. These dogs have no balance in their lives and they obsess over the woman they are with. Women become their only possession."

"The issue of sex is much different for women. Women tend to see sex as an act of love and being close to someone who nourishes her heart – maybe her commitment is very short term, but still the man that comes into her life and makes her feel loved or special and nourishes her heart will usually end up having sex with her."

'A woman's heart is a like a glass, she needs it to be filled with love. Where men can start wars and battles and sail around the world, women have the need to connect and feel nourished. In many ways she wants a man to fill her emotional glass with something good."

"Many women complain when dogs have hobbies that take them away for her or their family. In a way, maybe she is better off when he is busy and occupied with either work or hobbies. If he has too much free time on his hands he will get into trouble. Anything positive that keeps the dog busy is probably better for him and better for you. I say, "Never let a dog roam too far off the leash."

"So how do we deal with dogs who think of women as possessions?" Alicia questioned.

"Men are really much more insecure than women realize. Think of it like a man would think. He knows he has this beautiful girlfriend and all the other men are going to be trying to hit on her and pick her up. Even if she is just out with her girlfriends, he knows that guys will approach her and try. Men know how other men think. Whether she has a wedding ring on or she tells them that she has a boyfriend. It's not going to matter. Her dog is going to picture in his own mind that some other guy is trying to steal his girl. No matter how much she tries to reassure him, he is going to feel insecure."

"So if the guy is not treating his girl well, what you're saying is to go ahead and fuel his own insecurity and not call him or tell him who we are with and what we are doing?" Alicia questioned.

"Yes, it's okay to let a man become insecure, because he will cherish that love even more when it returns to him. Men are bad about taking advantage of a woman's love."

"Remember as women we want our love and time to be appreciated and if he is failing in that area then we have a duty to send very small messages that might make him think about what he is doing."

"Most women give insecure dogs way too much attention in an effort to reassure them that they will not leave. They reassure them without getting the results they want. For example, when women go out with female friends, they often call their dog to let him know she's thinking about him or to let him know she is home and alone."

"My friend Karen did something like that the other day. Her husband has been going out on the weekends with the guys. She decided to go out one night with her girlfriends. Her husband called her 15 times an hour. He was driving himself crazy thinking of her being out with the girls. She didn't take any of his calls, she just let him sweat! How do you deal with a relationship like that?" Alicia asked.

"My first suggestion would be that when a woman goes out, she simply says she's going out and not tell the dog where she is going or who she's going with. Be mysterious. Be aloof. And for heaven sakes don't call him or answer the phone while you are out. Many times the dog will call while you are out just to see if you answer and what you are doing. The more insecure he feels the more he will try to figure out what you are doing and who you are with. Don't rush to reassure him when you get home. Reserve the right to be distant and make him try harder to obtain your attention and reassurance that you are so crazy about him that you would never leave or look for another guy."

"But Julia this could be very bad advice I had a friend who had a horrible relationship with an obsessive man and actually having tried your similar advice. I can honestly say it only fueled the insecurity and led to him being more covert, spying secretly, from checking my cell phone call log to having others following her."

"It was the beginning of an end that turned violent. Obsessive relationships don't work because there is no balance in the relationship whether it is the man who is obsessive or the woman. They will both inevitably end up being miserable. There is no dealing with someone who is obsessive."

"I would agree there are some dogs that need to be taken to the city pound and given away. I am speaking more to the time in the relationship with a man when the relationship is developing in an understanding of how the relationship is going to be defined between a man and a woman. A woman has to see the earlier signs of problems in the relationship with a man."

"Early signs of a dog that is not trainable would be one that no matter what you try to get him to do, the dog has to be in control. There is no give or take in the relationship. He tries to cut the woman off from her friends and family. He might try to control her ability to work or transportation or her mobility."

"So why do women allow this?" Julia was surprised.

"Initially the dog makes her feel loved and safe"

"In the early stages of the relationship he finds a woman who needs his love, he promises much and makes her feel special. In this very special time she compromises the things she believes and makes his love more important than maybe it should be."

"There are bad dogs out there. There are dogs every woman should stay completely away from. There are dogs that bite. I am really trying to address the interaction that happens before a relationship gets that far."

"Dogs will play games trying to figure out who their rivals are and how you feel about him. Dogs are always trying to obtain and win. Make them work for your attention and affection. Don't give reassurance so easily"

"Dogs create bad images in their own minds, rather than looking at the reality of the situation. Research has shown that when dogs find out that their mate has cheated, they tend to obsess with the image of her being intimate with the other dog. They create an image in their mind and find it difficult to get rid of. I suggest that women let it run its course and only give reassurance when she is sure that he is not taking her for granted and is not making her a small piece of a big puzzle. She should wait until she is a larger, more important part of his life."

"Are we talking about how to train men?" Alicia asked.

"No! We're talking about training dogs!" I said as we laughed.

"But surely these same rules don't apply to married women. Relationships are much different for a married woman right?" Alicia said.

"Yes, I totally agree. In a good relationship with a dog, one where there is mutual love and respect, less training is needed. Some dogs are just naturally better and more affectionate than others. There are the Poodles, the German Shepherds and the Pit Bulls. But even in a marriage, there are issues which can range from mild to worse."

"In a marriage, some dogs make sure his wife is tied down with the children all the time. There is no opportunity for her to have free time, a woman will often try to please him by bending and bending until she is ready to break and becomes totally frustrated. What I'm saying is that she should MAKE free time for herself - MAKE him take the children some of the time or find a babysitter and not allow him to control her. She must take back some control over her life."

"Women are always trying to connect. If there is a liability to being a woman, it is the inherent need to connect to other people. I'm not sure if dogs have this same type of need."

"I've always been amazed at how women who have children seem to have a bond with other women who have children. This shows in their interactions with each other."

"Yet, if you have ever really listened to dog's conversations you will notice that they are often trying to see who can brag the most or who has accomplished the most. Maybe it's the alpha personality trait of dogs; they all want to be the best. They all want to conquer. They all want to be the TOP DOG! This is the dog mentality. Men really ARE dogs!" I laughed.

"So women have a need to connect and men don't have this same need?" Alicia repeated.

"No, dogs really don't have this same need. When women ask for advice on their relationship with a dog I tell them to do something that is very difficult for them."

"What is that?" Alicia asked.

"I tell them to find other things to make themselves happy - to exercise, to dance, to study, to read, to go out with friends...etc. Women should find their own way to happiness without a dog. A good man . . . excuse me, I mean a good dog will catch up to the woman as she continues on her own journey in life. An un-trainable dog might catch up for a day or so, but will soon wander off in another direction. A good dog will find her and join her on her path of life. As women we have to make ourselves happy first. The more secure and happy we are with ourselves the more happiness we have to share when someone does come into our life.

"So all untrained dogs stray?" Alicia smiled.

"Yes, I think all dogs want to stray. This is part of the reason we call them dogs. We want to believe that our dog will not stray. This is why we are surprised when he does. Yes, I think all dogs are born with this desire to stray.

"So is it possible to keep dogs from straying?" Alicia looked hopefully."

"Yes, absolutely, but first you have to realize that he is capable of straying and probably has a deep desire to stray. But the dogs will not often wander away from home when they realize what could be lost. His fear of loss is greater than anything he can gain by straying into someone else's backyard."

"You mean I have to put up one of those invisible fences around my yard that tells my dogs that if he wanders off his own yard he is going to get one of those electrical shocks?" Alicia chuckled.

"Yes, I guess I am exactly saying that!"

"Let's go back to the idea that each dog has a puzzle that represents his life. Let's say that he is married to a very beautiful woman who is a very large piece of his puzzle. This woman has his child and is desired by other dogs who often tell him how lucky he is to have her in his life. He knows, in his heart, that he is lucky and that he will never be able to get a woman like her again. He realizes that if he strays she will leave him. She will just get rid of her dog for a better one, if he fears the reality of losing her, he will think twice about screwing up the most precious piece of his puzzle."

"I know this couple. She is extremely beautiful with a great personality. She married a guy who was pretty average looking guy but has a kind and gentle heart. There is no doubt in my mind that this guy will not stray. He knows deeply in his heart that he will never be able to obtain another wife as nice, as beautiful and as loving as she is to him. In other words, he realizes there are so many other men that would love to be in his place that he would not do anything in the world to screw up this relationship."

"When women stray, cheat and have to end their affair, they often grieve the loss for between six months to two years. The typical dog will only grieve for a week or two. It doesn't mean as much to him as it does to her. When a dog cheats on a woman, she often blames herself and wonders what is wrong with her.   When a woman cheats on a dog, he obsesses over seeing her with the other man; this imagery drives him crazy as he pictures his rival with his object or possession."

"Damn, we women do care and love so much deeper than those dogs. I can't believe they can get over a woman so quickly." Alicia exclaimed.

"Statistically a dog that loses a woman, who is the biggest piece of his puzzle, is more likely to kill himself over the break up. Women are more likely to feel the emotional pain for a long time. Dogs are more likely to inflict pain on his self and her over the breakup. Dogs tend to strike out and women tend to hold the hurt in their own hearts. Dogs hate to lose what they think they own."

"Last year, I knew three men, who ranged in ages from 21 to 55, who after losing the woman in their life, their possession, and the focus of their attention killed themselves."

"Wow, that's terrible." Alicia said, sobered by this statement.

"Sometimes I think men just have a much more difficult time dealing with their emotions so they strike out in anger and frustration when they suffer loss. Especially the loss of someone they love so much. I think men know how to obtain but not how to maintain."

"So those dogs really do care about us… just not in the same way we care about them." Alicia said.

Chapter Two

"Training That Dog"

"But, I don't really want to have to TRAIN a man...well, a DOG, Julia!" Alicia said.

"You say that, but I have heard you as recently as last week talking to your boyfriend on the telephone and heard things that show me that this isn't really true."

"What do you mean?" Alicia was surprised.

"When he hung up quicker than you felt he should have, you called him right back and let him know that you felt he was too quick to hang up and asked him to take it slower... You appreciate him more if he takes the time to say "good bye" before hanging up."

"So you're saying is that I was really training him when I expressed my feelings of not being happy? Alicia laughed.

"What you were really saying was that this dog has potential, that he is trainable! I remember that other boyfriend you had. He was cheap and always asking you to pay for everything. Then there was the one who was rude and always hurting your feelings. Then there was the one who could not keep his hands off of other women. You dumped these guys, because no matter how much you loved them, you realized that you could not train them to be a good and faithful dog. Some dogs just cannot be trained to be a good partner. These are the dogs that you are thinking of when you say that you don't want to have to train them. But women are always trying to train their dogs."

"I am not sure I completely understand what you are saying. How do you feel we are always trying to train our dogs?"

"Women approach love much more differently than men do. The way men love is like a puzzle, which they are constantly trying to put together. Women's approach to love is much more complex and much deeper."

"So we're back to the electricity?" Alicia said.

"The way a woman loves is much more complex. But I think I can demonstrate it with these two coffee cups. If I hold one of the cups in my right hand and the other in my left hand and then slowly move them closer together. Now, I slowly move them farther apart and then closer together. After a few minutes, I move them farther apart again."

"Women try to move the two cups closer together. She tries to get closer to the people she loves. When she doesn't feel her love and loyalty and support returned, or she doesn't feel like the cups are moving closer to each other, she starts to question if the dog really loves her."

"Women want a good, faithful dog. When the dog does not demonstrate these qualities, she questions the space between herself and the dog - the relationship. Actually, women often question the space between two objectives. We drive ourselves crazy trying to figure out what we mean to others. Women want to "define the space". The problem is that space is abstract. It's very hard to define. This desire to define the space between themselves and others is part of what makes women so complex."

"You mean women see relationships as space between two objects?" Alicia said considering this idea.

"Yes, if you really look at the term "relationship" it means "being able to define the space between two people and identify what they mean to each other". But women are really the ones who focus on understanding their relationships."

"Women are always asking themselves the questions, does he love me? Does he love me more? Does he want to be with me? Is he losing interest in me? Why didn't he buy me a gift, or why didn't he ask me out? But women do not do this with just men. They do it with everyone in their lives."

"Men look more at what object, or woman, is in their puzzle as the object of their attention. Is she beautiful? Does she admire me? Does she want to do the same things I wants to do? Does she want to have sex? Will she make my life run better? In a nut shell this is how men think. For men it's about how much they can get. For women it's about understanding how important they are to the other person."

"As women we really listen intently to the words of a man to determine how important we are to them. When we feel like a man is lying we get upset because we know that if he is lying about the small things, he is probably lying about the big things also. We, as women hate it when men lie, if he will lie, he will cheat. The more honest he is, the more loved we feel."

"Men lie and cheat! The greatest destruction for a woman is that it makes her feel unloved. When he cheats, we equate that with "he doesn't love me" we lose trust in his words and actions!"

"I knew this woman who was married for twenty years, then she finds out that her nice, sweet husband of all those years had actually cheated on her as early as the first year of their marriage. Finding out he had been unfaithful devastated her. She went back and thought about all the love he had given her over the years and now she discounts the love she received. She cannot trust the love she received from him because of the lying and cheating. How could he really have loved her and done this?"

"Don't you think that men feel this same way about lying?" Alicia probed.

"No I don't. I think that as long as a woman is in the relationship and having sex with a guy he is more likely to forgive her for anything she might lie about. Remember men think in terms of possessions. So as long as the object is still there he is not as worried about how she acts, unless he thinks he has a rival who might steal her away. Men can go crazy when they think a woman is lying about having another lover. But overall, I don't think men are as concerned about a woman lying. Women can get away with almost anything as long as they keep having sex with their man and no other."

"Oh, that's bad. You are making women sound so bad." Alicia exclaimed!

"Come on! We know we are smarter than men and that we can run circles around them. I am just explaining WHY we can run circles around them. We are always on guard and listening for truth and lies. We question much more than men and look for details in what they say or don't say in a conversation. What makes us smarter is also what drives us crazy. We are constantly trying to decipher what they are really doing or saying.

"When a woman loses confidence in the faith and truthfulness of a man's words, his love fails to nourish her soul as much as it once did. When a relationship starts, women put a huge value on the love that the man gives her. His love might nourish her soul and heart. But the more the dog does to make her feel like she is not loved and special to him, the less he feeds the love meter in her heart."

"LOVE METER!" Alicia laughed. "You just made that up!"

"Yes. Her life, her childhood, the years of growing up and dealing with life is like a "love meter" - an invisible need to be loved. She might meet some guy who fills her heart and makes her feel special. But the more things he does wrong in the relationship, the less special she feels. Remember, a woman's heart is like a glass. A guy gives her love and fills the glass with life giving nourishment."

"Love, the most essential ingredient on earth..."

"That's a little dramatic don't you think?" Alicia said doubtfully.

"No. Not really. Think of all the crazy things people do for love. How many murders have occurred in domestic disputes where one side feels rejection and arguments heat up to such a degree that one kills the other. Most times the man will threaten to kill the woman. Women get upset at what is going on in the relationship and they voice their lack of approval. When a man's emotions explode it is much more dangerous with the adrenaline that increases in their bodies.

Unfortunately they have less ability to handle their own anger. Since they struggle to even understand the concept of how a woman is trying to define the space or the idea God might have made them stronger physically but they are no match for the sharper, verbal skills of a woman."

"I don't think men fully understand that if they disappoint a woman too much, their ability to nourish her heart might completely fade away. When the love that a woman receives from a man no longer nourishes her heart, he becomes more and more irrelevant to her love meter."

"Do you think men or women get over the break up quicker? Alicia wondered.

"Everything I have read on the topic says that men can get over relationships in several weeks and just focus on replacing the woman they lost with a new woman or object of attention. Women, however, can take anywhere from one to two years to fully get over the loss of a relationship."

"Let me explain in another way how women love. Think of a man's love as being a huge fire. A woman has a natural need to be warmed by a fire. The fire represents the love that a woman needs. Whether this love is from a man or this love is even another woman. Each woman still has that need to feel the warmth of another individual in her life."

"Weather is a good example of the changing feelings of a woman. This determines whether she does not really need to be warmed because the sun is out in her life. There might be many positive things going on in her life. These could be her hobbies, her career, her traveling to different places in the world."

"So a woman comes closer to the fire. This might be the person who nourishes her soul. Who makes her feel special, a person who fills her life and creates a warm glowing feeling inside of her heart. She is warmed by the fire. Yet, some relationships might pull her too close to the fire and she gets burned. She feels scared from the experience and has burns that cover her body and run deep into her heart."

"Yet, if she is too far away from the fire, the other person might not be meeting her needs and wants and desires. She ends up not feeling the warmth and love that this person provides."

"So men have gone from being big dogs to being a big inferno of fire that burns a woman alive?" Alicia said sarcastically.

"Well, think about it, the real secret of most all relationships is deciding where you stand? Stand too close to the fire and a woman gets burned. Too far away and the relationship provides no real warmth. Then there are days that the sun is shining bright outside and she could care less about a fire at all."

"Can I change fires and just put one out?" Julia asked.

"Women do change fires, when the flames don't burn strong enough or are trying to burn too many logs and too many women trying to be warmed by the same flames of the fire."

"Those men ARE dogs!" Alicia laughed and excused herself from the table.

"I will be right back, but I do have another question. Are men good listeners?"

Chapter Three

A Dog's Ability to Hear

"Can men hear very well?" Alicia asks her friend Julia as the waiter was taking their order for lunch.

"Well, they sometimes can. But I don't think they hear for the right reasons. A dogs hearing is great when it has to do with something he wants to do. When he has a task or objective that he really cares about his hearing is wonderful. But male dogs have selective hearing."

"One of the greatest needs of a woman is the ability to express her thoughts and feelings. A woman's need to communicate has long been recognized as one of her greatest needs in a relationship. However, many times books and speakers never tell us why she has this need. The answer is that it helps her to add meaning to others in a way that tells her that she is either important to that person or not important. Communication enables her to define her relationship – Relationships are really the space between herself and someone else. Remember, Relationship means the space between a woman and others.

"It is through communication that a woman deciphers how a man feels about her. She will often not trust that making love demonstrates his love for her, because, for dogs, the act of sex is not always about love. Especially if he proves to be a selfish lover - the type of dog that doesn't think about pleasing a woman and just wants to take care of his own needs. But there are other ways that he can express his love for her. He does this by being helpful; by picking up his clothes, doing dishes, buying her gifts, spending time with her, taking the trash out or paying the bills each month. Whatever it is, there are things that a dog will do that let her know he loves and cares about her. But more importantly it is her ability to define this space, this relationship between herself and the man she has expressed an interest in being a part of his life, both words and actions matter."

"So you're saying that these are the reasons a woman puts such emphasis on communication?" Alicia asked.

"Yes, a woman is always looking for ways to define the space between herself and her lover or person of interest. Words help her to define that space more than anything else. Without communication she can feel lost. Words mean everything to a woman. Once a dog has lied to her she no longer trusts his words. If she cannot trust his words, she cannot trust his love."

"Do men really hear a woman when she speaks?" Alicia posed the question again.

"No, I don't think they do. When a dog is out on a date with a woman he knows that his chances of getting lucky are better if he pretends to be listening to what she says. So he responds a little bit and shakes his head up and down. He just agrees with everything she says."

"So you're saying that they are pretending they are listening but they don't really hear what she says?" Alicia said with disappointment.

"Dogs do not have the ability to really listen. They are often thinking things like, "I wish she would just stop talking and have sex with me." If it's early in the dating he is often thinking, "Damn I wish she would let me move closer" or he is wondering if he'll get lucky. He is thinking about how to use the information she offers, in order to improve his odds of having sex. Sex is really all he's thinking about."

"Julia, you are not giving men credit for being anything but dogs!" Alicia exclaimed.

"Dogs make an effort to spend time with a woman they are interested in having sex with. They do this to acquire her. Sex is the objective and the most important part that allows a man to really know that she does really care about him and being a part of his life. So they find it difficult to really listen to what she has to say. And women often sense that men are not really listening."

"A friend of mine will stop in the middle of talking to a guy and see if he can remember what she just said. Or, she will ask him to tell her where she was in the conversation. She told me that it's amazing how dumbfounded the guys are when she asks a question about what she just said."

"Good for her, at least she realizes how badly they really do listen."

"As women we have a need to share and have mutual conversations. The only real way we can have our feelings validated is by sharing them with someone who truly listens in a non-judgmental way and genuinely cares. If a woman feels that she is not being judged or condemned, she is more open to sharing even more about her life."

"Women tend to feel more judged than men do. A woman worries about the labels others will place on her for her actions."

"You mean men or woman might call her a slut or whore if she does the same thing a man does?" Alicia nodded knowingly.

"Exactly, I read an article that said that the average woman would cut in half the number of men she had had sex with if she was talking to someone else about her sexuality."

"So they were both lying?"
"The dogs don't do that?" Alicia nodded.

"Are you kidding me? The dogs double the number, to make it appear they are more desirable and charming. Tell me this is not a double standard."

"When a woman finds a man or even a friend who does not judge her past, or her exploits, she feels more accepted. We all are looking for acceptance whether it be from other people or acceptance that our own actions are not inappropriate. We look for self-acceptance; in that acceptance there is freedom. This allows a woman to have freedom and not worry about other people's judgment."

"In acceptance from another person whose attention and time we value, there is freedom from worry about problems surfacing from the past."

"Yes. There is a double standard in the world. Consequently, women feel the need to hide things that dogs or others will judge or not accept. Sometimes these secrets can include rape, (which happens more often that what the statistics show). Women often blame themselves for things that might have led up to the act of rape. This can even include both physical and emotional child abuse. Yet, no matter how much is hidden in a woman's closet, she sometimes has a deep need to be accepted for her past."

"But Julia, can you really blame woman for not wanting to share that information?" Alicia was surprised.

"I had this female friend who thought she had met a great dog. After several months they took a trip to Colorado. As they were hiking in the mountains they stopped to rest along the path and her man pulled out an engagement ring and asked her to marry him. She was very excited, but realized that there was one thing she had not told him about her past. She never mentioned to him that she had once been married for six months before having the marriage annulled."

"She wished that she had told him earlier in the relationship but had never felt like the time was right. Now, as he proposed, she felt she had to tell him. As she told him the truth, she stated that he was welcome to withdraw his proposal. She held her breath as she waited for his answer, knowing that this was a test of his love for her. She prayed that it wouldn't matter to him that she had kept it secret that she had been married before thinking that if he really loved her. It would not matter to him.

"Did it matter?" Alicia asked.

"Yes, He took the ring back that he had just offered her. She was crushed that it had mattered to him that much. They ended the trip early and that was the end of the relationship. Apparently he could not deal with the idea of his woman actually being married to someone else. Its this type of double standard that many times keeps a woman from sharing what she might perceive to be a secrets of her past"

"Men! They wonder why we call them dogs!" Alicia was exasperated.

"There is power in being able to share where a person has been and have it validated by someone else. To cherish the past without fear or concern that it will be used against us is a very important thing."

"Women have a need for deeper emotional intimacy - to share experiences, dreams and goals. To know what her partner wants out of life and that their paths are the same - to be able to walk the path of life together and support each other instead of heading in different directions."

"A woman often thinks 'Can I share how I feel? Can I express my feelings and emotions and know that they will be received and validated?' Many times, once the feelings are expressed they disappear. When we share sadness, fears and even anger it helps it go away. Sharing the emotions helps women connect with the other person. Two individuals bearing their feelings is an important part of building a relationship. Intimacy is the act of two becoming one in the heart, soul and spirit."

"Think of it like this. Sometimes there are bad childhood memories. These memories get pushed to the back of our minds. Let's say that a dog comes into a woman's life and she feels like she can trust him. So she starts to share what happened in her past. She feels a bond developing as she shares more and more. She begins to build trust in him. But if he uses this information against her in an argument, or uses it to control her or have sex with her, she will lose trust in him. This may also cause her to be distrustful of others as well. She might find it harder to share with the next person who comes into her life and her closet of secrets closes its door more tightly. This can prevent her from sharing with those who would be good for her - the people who do care and can validate her feelings and give her the love she needs."

"So what about getting professional help?" Alicia asked.

"Well, don't get me wrong. I think professionals have a place in helping us heal and gain some insight. But, in the back of our minds, we realize that we are paying the person for listening to us. This is evident when the person looks down at their watch and prepares to end the session and move on to the next patient."

"So you don't think seeing a professional can help at all?" Alicia raised an eyebrow.

"I do think there is a place for them. I think they can help a person to understand what is going on inside them. I think they can help a person learn to cope with past events and learn to move past them. But I also think there is a power in someone we care about validating and accepting our deepest feelings and fears. In this act, we gain freedom from the past and are more able to move on to the future. In receiving acceptance from others we can gain acceptance in ourselves. Professionals tend to not be close enough to give this."

"So if men don't listen very well, how can women share their deepest fears and secrets with them?" Alicia was confused.

"Remember when I said "the scariest words to a dog are when a woman says; "We need to talk" because a dog often feels that he's done something wrong. It's difficult for dogs to face their own shortcomings. They don't really understand what is important to women, because dogs don't define the space between two objects. All they really know is that the object of their attention is either there and having sex with them or isn't. To him it's all pretty simple. Dogs hate to have "a talk". They really don't understand women's need to talk. As women, we think they should be just like us, but they aren't.

"So, how do we get them to do the things that would make a relationship better?" Alicia said.

"One way is to keep in mind that dogs don't like to be told to do things. They like to be in control. Their stubborn, childish ways will find a way to resist. But there are some suggestions that I might offer. A woman can make a list of the things she wants done and explain to him the priorities. Then if he accomplishes 50% to 80% of the things on the list, praise him and offer to do something for him that you would not normally do. For good acts give him a dog bone in the form of praise or something else that you know he wants. Give him a positive reward."

"What about the things he didn't do on the list."

"Don't focus on the fact that he didn't get everything done. Give him praise for the things he did right. Then put the uncompleted things on the next list, without complaining about them."

"So what is the big deal when women complain? Sometimes it's the only way to get them to do something. I hate to have to nag. It seems like he should just do what he's supposed to do without me having to ask twice." Alicia exclaimed.

"Dogs accept complaining when they think they deserve it - when they have really screwed up. When they miss a woman's birthday or anniversary or an important occasion, or if they get caught somewhere they aren't supposed to be, dogs know when they're in trouble. I think they are usually willing to accept the consequences of their actions."

"Dogs have a problem when women start to show more concern about smaller and smaller details of their daily life together. The smaller the incident, the more irritated a dog becomes until he wants to rebel because of what he perceives to be her unjust comments. Most women don't seem to realize how damaging her comments might be to the dog."

"Women often make the mistake of thinking that their words meant to bring the couple closer together have the exact opposite influence on the relationship. (Remember a dog doesn't understand this defining of space, so this whole argument is lost on him.) A dog just hears that he is doing something wrong and starts to think that no matter what he does she is not going to be happy."

"So you think complaints are dangerous for the relationship?" Alicia asked.

"Absolutely! I think if it's taken to the extreme there can be many very negative consequences. Women are sometimes even assaulted by their dogs in the heat of such a conflict. I can't help but wonder, every time I hear about the death of a woman at the hands of her mate, how much of it had to do with the lack of a dog's ability to handle a verbal conflict. You must realize that when it comes to arguing, dogs are at a severe disadvantage of the verbal skills of a woman."

"Well, that's kind of a scary!" Alicia said with surprise.

"Yes, I totally agree. Women often use their mental superiority over the big bad dogs they happen to live with."

"OK. Let's move on to another topic. My boyfriend and I were discussing me having male friends. I told him that there wasn't anything to it if they are just friends. What are your thoughts on this?" Alicia probed.

Chapter Four:

Can Dogs and Cats Be Friends?

"Hmmm..... There might be situations where dogs and women can work together. I personally believe that it's very hard for dogs and women to hang out together as just friends. It's difficult for a dog to spend his spare time with a woman or go out with a woman without thinking of her with some sort of romantic interest or possible conquest. As far as having dog friends that you go to the movies with, or go dancing or running with . . . no I don't think it's a good idea. I think that the issue of sex will eventually come up if it hasn't already."

"I don't agree with you! I have guy friends that I am not interested in having sex with" Alicia said indignantly.

"Let's go back to how women define the space between people. Imagine that a dog comes into your life. You find a label for this space between yourself and him. You might call him "just a friend." You might call him "a friend with benefits" a lover, a boyfriend, a fiancé or maybe even someday, a husband. But in all these instances we are just using labels to define the space between ourselves and another individual."

"Men don't do that!" Alicia was starting to understand.

"Dogs equate their time with effort, which is about obtaining the object of their attention or in having sex with them."

"You really think that all men want is sex?" Alicia said with some disappointment.

"Well, I think they think that is all they want. Ha! Ha! I realize that I sound like a man basher. But, I really am not. I'm just looking at the way dogs really think. Dogs will do crazy things to be close to a woman they are really attracted to. They often call it a friendship when, in fact they have other hidden agendas. I know it sounds crazy but I have even noticed at the grocery store how dogs will change the aisles they are walking down and repeatedly come down the same one as me, while pretending they are looking for something, when they are really just trying to connect with me."

"I wonder how many times women could look in a store window or a mirror and realize that men have turned around just to look at her butt"

"Men go out of their way to be around a woman they are interested in obtaining or wanting to have sex with. When they lose that interest, they go off in some other direction."

"Once I got a flat tire and was stranded on the side of the road, I had two dogs stop to help me change the tire. It was raining and I sat in the car while they got soaking wet. I wondered if they would have done the same thing for me, if I had been 5 feet tall and weighed 260 lbs."

"That is so true. You know I have noticed that men will find any excuse in the world to be around me. They will come up and ask me questions. They will offer to do the do things for me. Sometimes I think its natural and then I realize there are others that they are ignoring and I start to feel a little guilty about it. It can be both annoying and flattering. Alicia said nodding her head."

"Dogs do that. They find excuses to get closer. Never trust a dog that is really just looking for a way to get fed."

"Here is what I think. When a dog finds a woman, he thinks they have a pretty good chance of something happening. But if a woman tells him she has defined the relationship as being "just friends" he realizes that his chances have just diminished. He doesn't always give up completely. With the label "just friends" the dog realizes that the woman might change her mind. I must admit that we do some pretty fickle things. Dogs will do things to get closer, even if it's just being a "friend" when the truth of the matter is they are still interested in having a serious relationship, which involves sex."

"Dogs are really stupid, sometimes. But being the dogs they are they can also be cunning. They say that they just want to be friends but it really means they are trying to get closer. They are hoping a woman will change her mind or her mood will change. Think about how many dogs and women go to the bars and clubs as friends and after a little bit of drinking, the woman changes her mind and something ends up happening."

"Do you think men really do plan those things to happen?" Alicia asked.

"Dogs know that if a woman is drunk he has a much better chance of having sex with her. I admit that some dogs can even look better when I've been drinking heavily. Hee! Hee! "

"I guess dogs know that we can be a bit fickle with our emotions and they try to take advantage of it. Dogs seem to think that the longer they hang out with a woman, the better their chances get. They will eventually give up if it's not leading to sex. Dogs rarely complain about the time they've spent with a woman when it leads to sex, but if this doesn't happen they will often pull away. Sometimes they pull away just to see if we care. We can expect that at some point a dog who is just a friend will pull away to see how much we care about him."

"Some women become so dependent on a dog's attention that they will do almost anything to keep from losing that attention. Even if it comes with a higher price of her having to change the things she believes in, just to appease him. I think, as women get older and smarter, we start to figure out how men manipulate us. It's funny when we realize they are more like little boys than dogs."

"So what do you recommend when a man pulls away like that?"

"Let him go. He will come back. The male body has a need to procreate. His body and the desire to be close will probably bring him back in a couple of days. His male pride might slow him down but his biological needs will make him want to find a way to return. I must repeat, dogs may say they are just being friends but given the opportunity if they were really honest they would jump on just about any pretty woman, even if it was his best friend's wife or girlfriend."

"Wow, don't you think your being really harsh on men?" Alicia asked Julia earnestly.

"I believe that the more money, fame or power a dog has the more likely he is to be unfaithful. It's hard enough on those dogs that have none of those things...ha, ha! Most dogs have no idea what monogamy is."

"We act so appalled when someone tells us that somebody's husband cheated on her. We act like it's the worst thing in the world. Yet, every time I ask where it started, nobody seems to know."

"You don't even believe in monogamy?"

   "I do believe in monogamy, just not for the same reasons most people do. Okay, here is how I see it. Most people have no idea where the concept started, or why. When I look at the world I see many cultures where people can have one or more spouses. I read about adultery and have no idea which one is right or wrong. The statistic varies a great deal. I feel certain that monogamy is not practiced as much as most people would want to believe. But here is the point I always come back to... I think people want to believe that their love is special. They want a connection to someone else that values their love on both emotional and physical levels. That is why I believe in monogamy...not because someone has told me that it's the way I am supposed to live."

"I think that if people approached their relationships more realistically, they will understand the natural attraction that goes on between dogs and women and avoid situations that can lead to long term relationship problems."

"I will give you an example.... instead of getting up each day and assuming I will live forever and never die. I get up and live every day with appreciation that it was a gift. I treat that day as a gift - an opportunity to find love and enjoy life. Dogs and cats can be friends. But don't assume there will not be issues and moments of conflict and sexual tensions, especially if one of them is committed to someone else."

Chapter Five

"Leashing the Dog"

"Dogs see women as objects of their attention. They are visually oriented and this is very apparent in how they view women. Men will notice quickly if a woman is attractive to him. Men will notice and desire her, whether she is single or married. I do think most dogs try to respect the fact that a woman is married, but this will not stop all of them. In fact many will find it more exciting in pursuing her."

"Women understand that dogs are object oriented. They learn from an early age to make themselves more attractive to dogs. This starts as early as 11 and 12 years old. Women would love to believe that dogs are deeper and wiser than that, but dogs are just not that way."

"Dogs do not see the space between the objects. They do not even understand the concept. A dog is really much simpler. He sees her beauty, her legs, arms, eyes, hair, her figure and maybe even her smile. He sees what she LOOKS like. He is the hunter looking to "win" the object of his attention. A dog wants to be "admired". He wants the respect and admiration of the woman he is making an effort to win."

"The only time a dog understands how a woman defines the space between them is when she leaves the relationship. At this point the dog wakes up one day and she is suddenly gone, but he really doesn't understand what has happened, when he'd thought everything was okay."

"You mean the dog doesn't really get it? I could be telling him over and over that there might be something that he needs to do to make me happy and he doesn't understand that he needs to change his behavior?" Alicia continued with her questions.

"No, they really don't get it. Women can say something once, twice, three times, even over and over again, but eventually dogs go back to letting the relationship continue just the way it was. Dogs let it go in one ear and out the other for as long as she - the big bone, is still there in his life. Women; however, do have a breaking point."

"Though he has no idea why she wanted to leave the relationship, after she is gone his eyes begin to open. The only time a dog realizes this space between the objects is when it's gone. This is normally the point when a dog tries to figure out what went wrong in his relationship. Like a drifting stranger in the streets of love, he searches for answers."

"Now, let's go back to the idea about dogs being possessive. There are dogs who take the idea of the pieces of the puzzle to extremes. Let's say a dog has not accomplished as much as he would have liked to do in his life. He does not have the job or money or other things he'd wanted to have. But by chance the lucky dog ends up with a wonderful woman who believes in him. His life may start to revolve around her. Instead of having a balanced puzzle, he starts measure his life by her. She becomes the only piece to his puzzle. Without her, he feels like nothing. He starts to fear losing her and tries harder and harder to control the situation, so that she doesn't leave. Eventually, she might start to feel more and more irritated and upset because his control tactics can become too restrictive."

"What do you mean by control?"

"The core of "control" is when the dog develops a growing fear of losing his lover and places more and more restrictions on her in order to keep her from having fun with anyone else. But this also keeps her from growing as a person. After a while, the woman does not feel his love anymore. She feels that she has become a mere possession. There are some dogs who will not allow a woman to have a job or career, drive a car, or have any free time or any other sort of freedom. Some dogs cannot even allow their woman to go grocery shopping alone or to get their hair done without escorting her. Control places too many limits on the woman."

"Can you give me more examples?"

"Sure, I have a friend who noticed that every time she needed to go get groceries her dog would say "Oh, I'll come too." At first she thought it was sweet and that her dog just wanted to be helpful. Sometimes it would be in evening when she went shopping and she thought he was just being protective. Then she began to notice it wasn't just the grocery store it was everywhere she went. Whether it was to drop off mail at the Post Office or to treat herself to a manicure, her dog insisted on accompanying her. Eventually, she realized that the only place she went without being escorted by her dog was when she went to work every morning. Even then, he would call her around five minutes after she got off from work to ask where she was and how soon she would be home."

"Wow, that's pretty bad! What happened, are they still together?"

"Well, needless to say, it wasn't too long before she got fed up with his lack of trust and obsessive behavior and she found she had no choice but to end the relationship. But by then her dog's obsession was so strong that it was not a friendly parting, but a violent one. His need to control her only made it difficult for her to break free."

"Control is when a dog prevents his lover from doing what she wants to do; like not wanting her to open a business or go to meetings just because he is afraid that she might meet some other dog; or maybe he tries to prevent her from going to college or to a party without him by her side.

"Sometimes, the dog begins to feel he is losing control of his woman and his behavior becomes more exaggerated, more bizarre and can become extremely dangerous very rapidly. The more she tries to break free, the tighter he tries to hold on. The tighter he holds on, the more determined she becomes to break free. Someone is bound to snap in this kind of situation."

"So, the more he tries to control, the more he loses her?"

"Exactly, this type of control causes their whole relationship to diminish or disintegrate. The person who is being controlled starts to resent it. "Resentment" now that is an interesting word. Have you ever really thought about what RESENTMENT means?"

"No." Alicia shook her head.

"Well there are two words that seem to be on the opposite side of a fence. They are "Resentment and Guilt.""

"What do you mean?"

"We feel guilty when we are not measuring up to the expectations that other people have placed on us. Resentment occurs when others do not meet our expectations. The difference is between the two different sets of expectations. Guilt keeps us from doing certain things and resentment causes us to do certain things."

"Think of it like this…. life can be like two different sides of a scale. When we do things, that we feel guilty about, one side of the scale goes down until something happens to balance it out again. Resentment can be so great that it makes us want to do something out of hate toward the other person. Like getting pissed off when your partner is spending money while you are trying to save it, so you go out and spend a lot of money just to get even."

"So if one person starts to feel controlled and possessed they might resent it, rebel and do things like this?"

"Yes very much so, when you think about it, rebellion is an outward act of defiance when the control interferes with the love and good feelings that were initially intended. Even teenagers do that. They start to feel "controlled" more than they feel the love from their parents and then they rebel against them."

"So you do not believe that couples should control each other?"

"No, I believe in control"

"Oh! I am surprised! You do?"

"Yes, I believe that the strongest form of control is merely love. People will do anything for love. So that makes it the greatest form of control."

"I don't agree. Love and Control don't really go hand in hand with each other. So you are going to have to explain this one to me" Alicia sighed.

"You are thinking of control as being a bad thing. Yet we use the phrase self-control when we displace discipline - in not doing something that we think is bad for ourselves; like in eating correctly, exercising and maybe refraining from doing drugs or other activities that might not be good for us. Self-Control is when we overcome our own bad side to do what is right and good."

"But if someone really loves you in a pure and unconditional way, their love can be a form of control that encourages us to do the right thing. I love my children, so I refrain from doing wild and crazy things because I cherish their love and respect for me."

"Control can be used in crowds of people, in order to make sure they do not riot or go crazy. Control can be both good and bad. But one would have to admit that people do crazy things for "love". The need for love controls more of our actions than most of us want to admit. But many women hate the very idea of control, because dogs so often hurt them."

"I don't understand. Why so people strike out to hurt someone they are supposed to love?" Alicia asked.

"For dogs it's often due to the loss of that possession - the loss of being able to control what they view as their possession. This type of control is terrible. I often wonder how many murders and injuries have occurred because of arguments between dogs and women."

"Yes, I agree I cannot tell you how many times I pick up the newspaper and read stories of men who kill their girlfriends or wives and keep saying "I loved her."

"Seems like it would be easier just to try and make her happy." Alicia said.

"My girlfriend complains about her husband going out with the "guys" once a month and leaving her and the kids at home." So I told her to do the same thing to him. But don't answer the cell phone when he starts calling to see what she is doing. So you want to guess how many times he called her to see what she was doing?"

"Five?"

"More."

"Ten?"

"More. He called her twenty one times! Then, a month later, when her man would normally have gone out for a "boys" night out. He decided to take her out on a date instead of going. He realized that he could not stand the idea of her being out and not knowing what she was doing."

"When a woman starts to pull away from the man in her life it can be a very scary moment not only to her but also for him. This is especially true in some foreign cultures where control of the woman is more predominate than it is in American culture. This is the point that dogs can be the most dangerous. Especially if he was an extremely dominating and controlling dog who should have seen the warning signs but continued to act in the same way."

"In many ways women suffer pain worse than dogs. It is often the dog who inflicts the pain in her life. This happens to many women and children. Many have been raped and feel that they cannot share that news with even those they are close to. Yet, there needs to be more awareness of this problem. I think that if women refuse to be victims they channel the anger at those who try to make them victims."

"There is a hidden proposition about love. If you deeply love there will be pain. There can be no greater pain than to be separated from someone we love. And, eventually, there is always some form of separation, even if it is the final, yet eventual separation of death."

"That is a sad thought."

"I believe that where there are tears, there is love. So it's okay to hurt - to feel pain - to cry. Love, even with all the pain that might come from it, is the most miraculous and wonderful thing in the world."

"There were some things that happened to me when I was a very young girl; I find that I cannot talk about them to anyone. I am too embarrassed to discuss and in a way I don't think that anyone will understand what happened to me."

"Almost any woman who has had bad things happens to them as young girls believe that others will not understand and many times feel guilt and shame instead of the anger over what happened. They become victims and prisoners of past actions instead of sharing them."

"Not everyone can handle the truth or wants to discuss bad things." Alicia continued.

"I agree, but in a way it becomes even more important in a woman's life to find that person, whether it is a girlfriend, mom, sister or man who will listen to what happened and allow the woman to be released from the guilt she might be feeling over her past."

"Memories might fade over time but many times they don't really fade, but rather they hide in the soul of a woman, the deepest part of her there is a hidden secret. Like a room within a nice house that has a closet. In this closet is her deepest fear that she is afraid to open. She wants to share all the other rooms of the house except for this one closet because she is afraid no one else will understand."

"Yet, somehow the past events find a way to affect the present, and in the present many times we find ourselves trying to fix the very things that happened in the past. They become the emotional triggers that might upset us and others in our lives don't really understand because the reactions to the triggers are greatest that what one would have expected."

"So "triggers" are the events out of the past that we overreact to?"

"Most people would never want to know. Most people are just too shallow to care.

"Or if they are listening, all they really want is something from me."

"That can happen. I am not saying that all people deserve our trust. You give them a small piece of truth and if they can accept it, then you give them another one until they prove they don't deserve it anymore."

"Think about it like this Alicia, there are great events and bad events that happen in everyone's life. Good memories and bad memories."

"The good memories make us want to do those same activities again and again, while the bad events that happen in our life make us want to avoid them. Whenever we stop to think about the good memories or the bad memories we have many of the same feelings about those memories. Not to the same degree, to a much lesser degree, but we still find inside ourselves many of those same feelings from the past experiences and events."

"People are like cups. They fill their lives with good and bad memories. There is a need inside of us to want to share those memories and feelings."

"One day I was thinking about criminals in prison." Julia said seriously.

"What did you think?" Alicia responded smiling.

"I was thinking how when you have the very worse people in the world who are already prisoners and you want to punish them; you put them in isolation."

"Do Dogs have the need to talk or bark?" she said.

"Women have the need to communicate I think for men it's more the need for companionship." Julia responded.

Chapter Six

Women are the Center of the Universe

"Do you think men really know what it means to "make love and be in love?"

"No. A dog seems to think that making love is nothing but great sex."

"So you agree it's different for a woman?"

"I think women can divide sex into more categories . . . sex as a recreational activity, as an erotic spur of the moment thrill, as a bargaining chip, as making love."

"Do men really understand making love?"

or

"No. But let me spell it out. Being "in love" is when she can only see him and his love for her. For the dog, it's when a dog can see her and her love for him."

"Can you give me an example, Julia?"

"Sure, I can give you two examples. One goes back to the idea of two objects. Let's say two cups. I keep saying that women want to be close and connect. So if I move the two cups very close to each other and they are so close to each other those two cups (people) can only see each other."

Remember men see the object of his attention."

"So, for him it's being so close he only sees her. For a woman it's about how connected she feels to that other person."

"Also, remember I used the analogy of fire again. Think of the man as the fire. This is when a woman comes so close to the fire that she only feels the nourishment and love from one guy. A woman feels only his love, his warmth, only he touches on her heart."

"When she has this special feeling that is incredibly close to him that she can and does not want the love of any other man. Like in my example of the man being fire; being "in love" is when she feels close to the dog in her fire. The heart of a woman is like a cold night. She sees the warmth of the fire. This fire is the love she values. But like any fire, stand in the fire and the person is burned and destroyed."

"The secret to all relationships is trying to figure out is what is too close and what is too far away."

"Stand too close and the fire or love of a man can consume her, too far away from the fire and it does not make a woman feel cherished or loved. The key to all relationships is to understand the needs of the woman and the wants for that relationship with a dog. It is up to her to understand herself. Then she can figure out how close to stand to the "fire" (dog or man) in her life."

"Making love is just a natural result of being in love. It is both a physical and emotional union between couples. Making love is the total package of physical and emotional love. I think women understand this far better than dogs because they are more likely see it as a state of happiness for getting what he wants."

"After this state of being in love can a woman find herself occasionally still feeling depressed about the relationship Alicia?"

"It seems like women end up with more issues related to depression than dogs do. If you think about the way women define the space between themselves and dogs, and extend this same idea to relationships in general, it starts to explain why women suffer from depression more than dogs."

"If you think of a woman as being in the center of all the activities that go on in her life and the effect this has on her. Whether it be that she needs to be a good mother, a good daughter, a good wife, a good employee, a good boss. In essence she has to play so many different roles and has many tasks to juggle. In each of these roles there are people pulling at her to be something, provide something, and accomplish something. This pulls at her and her emotions. When she starts to feel overwhelmed she will start to push back and often start to withdraw from some of the activities that go on in her life."

"Many women do really well at balancing all those roles. But there are times that it can become overwhelming. She will want to withdrawal emotionally until she can figure out which ones are important and which one's she can eliminate."

"Depression is a direct result of the many burdens these roles have put on her and the emotional stress she feels towards having to keep them in balance and the pressure it places on her in keeping her world together."

"Sometimes I think women are more spatial even when it comes to houses, cars, and parking spaces."

"Parking spaces?' Alicia said quizzically.

"Yes, even parking spaces. Have you ever seen how women compete to get the parking space closest to the mall doors?"

"Yes, but there are practical reasons, it's safer. There are packages to carry and during the bad weather there is less distance to the car." Alicia argued.

"Yes, I totally agree. But dogs don't think like that. They are just glad to get a parking space and the objective is to get into the store, buy what they need and leave. I have seen women get upset that they had to park a little farther out and even wait for 10 minutes to get a parking space 30 feet closer to the door."

"I don't know that I totally agree but I do see your point." Alicia said skeptically.

"Let's assume that this defining of the space happens more in a woman's life than we realize. Let me give you an example. A woman is the center of the universe. She is at the center of her own special universe. She is the sun that all the planets revolve around."

"Women are at the center of the universe and everyone revolves around her. Her husband or boyfriend, her children, the people at her job, her parents...etc., all revolve around her. Since women question the space between themselves and others, they are constantly trying to figure out what they mean to the objects (or people) that move around her."

"Most of the time, women are great at juggling all these

moving objects. Women are so terrific at multitasking that men often just let them do it. But this can make us feel overwhelmed.   As we try to juggle more and more balls, inevitably we drop one to the ground. Once that rhythm is broken, more balls get dropped. We start trying to push some of those activities or objects (men or women) away. We feel more and more stretched and then start to resent our dog for thinking that we are a Wonder Woman or some type of Superwoman. Sometimes we just need our dogs to give us more help and support."

"However, not all women are the same. Some can handle more activities than others. But when women start to feel stressed they will want to slow things down or get more help. In this process she will often push people away until she can handle her world and it becomes more manageable."

"I can see it in my dance class. Women learn so much faster in the dance classes. The men don't seem to catch on as quickly." Said Alicia as she was starting to really understand the way those dogs danced in her class.

"Yes, I have noticed that as well. I think it's risky when it comes to relationships." Julia responded.

"What do you mean?" Alicia asked.

"Women who learn quickly can tend to offer too much advice to their dogs on how to do things. They call it 'Back Leading' in the class." Julia continued.

"What is back leading?" Alicia asked.

"Well, when you learn how to dance, the dog's role is to lead. Dogs have to learn to lead on the dance floor. But often women learn faster and in an effort to be helpful they start telling the dogs how to do things. The woman starts trying to lead the man in the right direction and what steps to take during a dance. Dogs have to learn how to lead. But if a woman is telling them what to do then they stop trying as hard and often give up, saying that they don't know how to dance. Dogs do not like women telling them how to dance. They feel insulted by it."

"So how do you get them to do it right?"

"Let them go slower and avoid the tendency to tell them how to do it. Be patient. And most importantly find something that they do right and praise them. I once had a partner and his timing on the dance floor was terrible. But he was good at turning and spinning. So I complimented him on that. I continued to encourage him in the things he did right and was amazed by how much better he got. The positive reinforcement helped him learn. I could still be the center of his world and let him be the leader."

Chapter Seven:

Questions about Love and Loving

. There are many differences between women and dogs. Here is an overview of them . . .

Dogs view work and money as a measurement of success in life.

Cats feel rejected when dogs ignore them, work too much or are gone too often.

Dogs think they are more logical, analytical and rational. Yet, the dogs are the first to want to start a war. Dogs are wired to go out and conquer, whether it is war, or exploring the world. Dogs do not seem to see the contradictions in thinking they are logical and misuse of that logic to bring negative results.

Dogs have fewer feelings as they relate to what is happening in the relationship.

Dogs might never really understand the relationship but can be far more devastated by its ending, since they have fewer friends they will discuss their loss with and fewer sources of emotional support.

Dogs think they are more functional in approaching problem-solving. Which is why when a cat is voicing problems, the dogs are replying with functional problem solving answers not realizing that might not be what is going on inside of the cat.

Cats are more aesthetically-oriented.

Dogs feel that women complain too much.

Cats feel that dogs don't listen enough.

Cats often give advice in order to improve the relationship.

Dogs, when told what to do, often perceive it as if they are being told that they aren't competent or don't know how to do things right.

Cats express emotions and longings to be closer to him.

Dogs feel responsible for her problems and often feel hopeless in being able to alleviate her sadness.

Dogs always assume that women want advice and solutions to problems. This is how they show affection.

Cats want the dog to sincerely listen.

Dogs will try to avoid housework, try to get others to do housework for them at all cost and find excuses not to do the housework. They even feel demeaned if told to do the housework. Inherent in a dog is the desire to not be, told what to do, even if he knows the cat is right. Ask don't tell or make demands.

Cats spend a great deal of time trying to change a man's behavior by offering unsolicited advice and criticism.

Dogs appreciate advice and criticism only when they request it.

Dogs like to feel like they are top dog and king of their own domains.

Dogs like to solve problems as long as they are not the problem.

Dogs need to feel important, have status and independence.

Cats need intimacy and an emotional connection.

Dogs need to receive appreciation, admiration, approval, and encouragement.

Dogs' deepest silent fear is that he is not good enough or not competent enough.

Dogs 'wannabe' big dogs are defined through the ability to achieve results and success.

Dogs can hunt alone or in packs.

Dogs are more interested in tangible objects and or things they obtain or accomplish.

Cats are more interested in people and emotions.

Dogs feel devastated by failure and financial setbacks.

Cats are more interested in the quality of the relationship.

"Julia. Just tell me, how do I find this trainable dog!" Alicia pleaded.

"How do I know if I have found a good dog or a bad dog - a trainable dog or an un-trainable dog? Help me understand the questions I should be asking, in order to find out the truth about him."

"Julia, tell me how to find a trainable dog." Alicia almost demanded as she repeated herself just wanting a checklist of how to know she might have the right dog?

"Okay. Let me think. Well, the questions I would ask myself are . . .

"Does he bring out the best in me?"

"What makes me feel proud when I am with this person?"

"Do I trust him to always tell me the truth?"

"Does he make me feel secure?"

"Can I be myself and relax around him? "

"Can I bare my emotions and be physically naked and feel that he cherishes and wants each part of me?"

"Do I pull away from him or want to embrace him?"

"Does he really listen to what I say?"

"Can we be together and not feel like we have to talk all the time?"

"Do we enjoy the same things?"

"Can we communicate easily?"

"Does he make me feel special?"

"Would he be a good father?"

"Are we both willing to share our time, money and energy for each other?"

"Can we find common ground and compromise when we argue?"

"Can I forgive him?"

"Do we have emotional intimacy?"

"Do our conflicts find resolution? Instead of fighting to win, can we find win/win solutions?"

"Can we honor each other without too much self-sacrifice?"

"Is the relationship mostly peaceful and fun?"

"Are we growing together or are we growing apart?

"Do we look forward to being together and miss each other when we are apart?

"Do we want to please each other?"

 "Does either of us feel like we are being controlled or manipulated?

"Is our relationship free of demands or threats?"

"Do we find acceptance and freedom in the relationship?"

"Is he loyal and supportive?"

"Wow! Those are pretty hard questions to answer. But they are good ones. What happens if my man doesn't meet all those specifications? Do I dump him?" Alicia asked eager to learn more.

   "Hell no! Don't dump him!" Remember that you're not trying to change him. What you're trying to do is to figure out if he is trainable - if you are working with good material or defective material? Change happens when the other person has the qualities above - when they want us to be happy. Don't buy the dog just to change him. Don't buy the dog because you need to have his attention. Buy the dog to share your life, your home, your happiness, your love and your joy. Don't just expect happiness to automatically be there for you. Take it with you. Then you don't have to worry about what awaits you!"

   "Dogs normally have a difficult time understanding why women get upset when it comes to things like Valentine's Day, Mother's Day, Birthday's, Christmas and Anniversaries. Dogs assume that if they just get them a gift everything should be okay. However, what a woman is really looking for is how much thought and effort a dog puts into the things he does. What she really wants to know is if he cares about her. It is not easy for women to define this space between herself and the person she cares about, yet, she will look for clues in everything he does to try to figure out whether he loves her or he is really just not that excited about her. For example a gift of jewelry or a sexy teddy speaks to women as "he really loves me, or he still thinks I'm sexy" where a new set of pots and pans sends a totally different message!" Julia said with a chuckle.

"Julia, I think I am getting the idea. Now I realize why my boyfriend just happened to buy me the exact same outfit for my birthday that I had in my closet. I was very upset as I wondered why he didn't notice." Alicia said as if a light bulb had just turned on.

"Oh Alicia that's nothing... Mine purchased twelve red roses and looked really pleased with himself until I pointed out that they were artificial flowers! My dog of a husband did not even notice."

"Oh no, he didn't do that!" Alicia exclaimed.

"I guess he felt more like a whipped puppy than a dog." They both laughed.

"For at least a week, he never acted better trained after that happened"

Our meal was winding down, Julia could see that Alicia wanted her to really put all that they had talked about in a more concrete and practical format. Finally, Alicia came out and asks the question. "Please go back to the idea of men being like a puzzle and explain to me exactly how do I figure out my man?"

Laughing I took out two pieces of paper and said. "Alicia with these two pieces of paper I can explain the fundamental differences between men and women."

I placed the two sheets down on the table. I labeled one of the sheets "the man" and on the other one "the woman".

"First, let me explain the life of a woman. I will place her in the center of the page. Then we have to figure out all the different roles she plays in her life. Whether she is a mother, whether she is a daughter? Is she a sister? Does she work? Does she have a husband or boyfriend? Does she have both?

"Oh, you are bad!" Alicia winked at Julia.

"Maybe, but we both know that women can be just as bad as men and have more than one man on the hook at the same time."

"Been there, done that …it makes life more complicated." Alicia sighed.

"Now, I want you to look at all the roles that a woman plays in her life. What we have to do is place them on page in relationship to how close or far away they are from her."

"So what I want you to do are to draw little circles on the page that represents her roles to others. How close is the circle to her parents? How close is the circle to her children?

"So now my life is reduced to little circles on the page?" Alicia shrugged.

"To understand a woman, a person has to understand what roles she is playing in her life and how close or important are these roles. One role a woman might play is that of being a Sunday school teacher or a kindergarten teacher. A woman might have several roles as a lover and girlfriend. The idea is to look at all the different roles she has going on in her life and to look at the ones that are close to the center of the page."

"You mean the ones that are important to her? What she considers her priorities?" Alicia was beginning to understand.

"Yes, the more roles she has the more complicated her life might be. A woman might enjoy the many roles she has until they become overwhelming and then she will start to eliminate those roles or objects in her life so she can slow down and define all the ones that are really important to her. The reality is that a woman is always trying to define that space between herself and others in her life and define those relationships."

"When they are in conflict she has to find a way to cope by reducing the number of objects circling around her life so she can define the ones that are the most important and must remain in her life."

"A woman's control is her ability to manage those many roles she has in her life and her ability to cope with all of the demands that result from those in her life."

"This is why women call out for help from her mate, the significant other person or people in her life. Why she notices the things he can do to help her manage the roles she has to play. She sees the roles and demands and tries to figure out how they will all work together. If she cannot work them out, and then she will try to eliminate them from her life."

"A male friend of mine jokes that women and men can be seen in the way they view cars."

"How is that?"

"Men will see a car and want to trade the one he has for a better car. He always wants to trade up."

"Women, when they think they have a broken car will just get rid of it. Even if they do not have a car to drive they will get rid of the broken one. Then they will try to find a way to get around. First, they dump the problem they have before finding a replacement."

"Men think the new car is the solution to all their issues..." Julia said smiling and joking with Alicia.

"But there is a lot of truth in that..." Alicia agreed

"Now the good part, let's figure out this idea of men."

"What I want you to do on this sheet, calling it "the man" is to write down everything that is really important to your man. These could be things like hunting, fishing, work, hobbies, family, the children, his mother or his father. Now one of the ways you look at what is important to him is the amount of his time that he gives to an item. Also, you might want to look at the money he has and where he spends that money. The combination of all of these items, how he spends his money and time are priorities that are his pieces of the puzzle. These are the pieces of his puzzle and help to create the image that he has of himself."

"Write everything that is important to him down on this sheet."

"Wow this is hard. It's hard to figure out what is important to him. I mean he does go to work but he doesn't really enjoy his job." Alicia said, with a frown wrinkling her forehead.

"Put work down on the list and then continue to think of other things that are important to him." Julia advised.

"He spends time at the church but he does not really like to go. I think he does it more just because he was expected to go by his parents. He loves to go hunting and spends weekend after weekend going with his buddies to hunt." Alicia continued making her list.

"Well, write it down on the sheet." Julia encouraged.

"Okay… I think I know a few more. He loves to see his mother and father and we end up spending at least a few days a month with them up in New Bern, North Carolina." Alicia added.

"Now what I want you to do is place a percentage on the items."

"What do you mean?" Alicia was really confused now.

"I want you to start at the top of the list and write a percentage based on importance to the item. How important is each item on the list?" Julia asked.

"But here is the catch. At the bottom of the list you cannot place more than 100% on the total list."

"You are really making this hard." Alicia groaned.

"Well, I would put his job up there high on the list maybe give it 40%"

"Hunting is important too. So I think I will give that 30%"

"Then children, car and maybe the house I would divide them up and give them all about 30% as well." Alicia continued.

"You can't lump them together what you have to do is assign a percentage to them. You have to break them down into what you really think he finds important." Julia interrupted.

"Okay, okay...but this is not easy…" Alicia groaned again.

Alicia returned to the page and finally assigned all the numbers to list.

"Now it adds up to 100% finally. So what do I do once I have them all assigned?" Alicia asked.

"Well you take the piece of paper and draw the pieces of his puzzle in proportion to how things are important to him. First you have to figure out is this a person who has a big puzzle or a small puzzle. Does he have many pieces to his puzzle or does it just have a few. This will help you see what things are important to him and whether he has so many things going on that other things get squeezed out and he does not make them a priority in his life." Julia said.

"What you are really trying to do is figure out his image of himself and what things are important to him." Julia continued.

"Okay...I get it. Let me draw the pieces on the paper...." Alicia focused on the paper again.

A few minutes passed as Alicia drew her man's puzzle on the paper.

Leaning back in her chair after the drawing of the puzzle... "Something is wrong with this puzzle." She said glumly.

"Yes, I agree but you have not figured it out yet?" Julia said already knowing the answer to problem.

"Me!" Alicia exclaimed when she realized. "I'm not a piece of the puzzle!"

"That's right, you didn't see yourself as being all that important in the life of your boyfriend. You have started to realize that maybe you are not as important to his life as you would like to be."

"Oh, I cannot believe that I did not think of this myself sooner. Maybe that is an indication that there might be an issue here."

"Yes, maybe it is an indication of an issue."

"I don't think I have ever felt like I am really as important to his life as I should be. This really helps drawing his puzzle. I can really see that I am not as important as I need to be!"

"Maybe this dog really isn't the right dog for me, life is such a puzzle!" Alicia exclaimed.

"Can you give me a for instance?" Alicia questioned.

'Men want acceptance, they are not really looking for a woman to try and completely change them. They want to stay as good as they were the day they got married. However, as women, we are always than trying to make them better. We notice more things in life then they do and understand how to make them better. Whether it is how they dress at work or the clothes they wear going out on date night. We just see more things and how they can be better.'

"What do you think is one of the biggest mistakes a woman makes in relationships?"

"

Women assume that their requests for a dog to do something that might seem reasonable to them and not a very big or important deal, will find many times that it not acceptable to the dog in their life."

"Can you give me an example?"

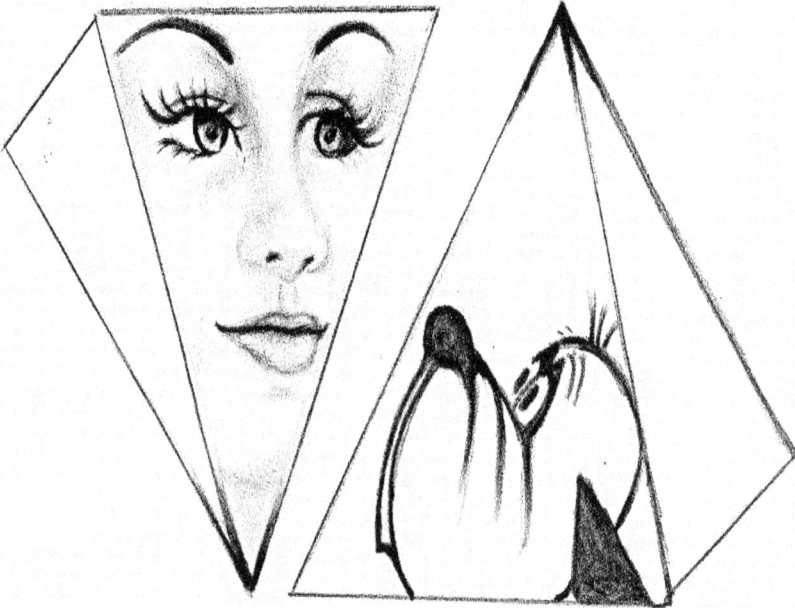

"When a dog makes a mistake; and he will make mistakes in his relationship with a woman. He really blows it in the relationship. He does something really stupid, like lose some money on a car or house. He goes out and gets drunk and does not go to work. The dog knows he can expect some nagging and a upset woman. He is prepared to take the verbal assault she lets loose on him for his actions. Surprisingly If he knows he messed up, he will accept his punishment.

But a dog, many times has a less favorable response to a woman on things that to him seem very small and trivial. When a woman enters the house and gripes at him for not putting his shoes up in the closet or picking up the clothes on the floor. Maybe she is upset he is not lifting the toilet seat in the bathroom. Women think these small acts of consideration just make the relationship better and closer. To a dog, he asks himself the question "if she cannot love me in the small details and she cannot accept me in the small things how is she going to accept me if I tell her more and bigger issues."

"Women assume their small comments do not hurt the ego of the dog and the truth is they can and do."

"This is why so many times men are willing to give in to the small details of lives with a woman and just let her go with things but for a woman to think these don't do some damage would be a mistake.

"How many arguments start and erupt over the littlest of details?"

"Dogs are not willing to change for the love of a woman?"

"Yes, I think the dogs are open to change and learning to some degree"

"Dogs are willing to change but only want to change 5% to 10% of their basic personalities. Women; however, tend to find guys that they want to change far more than that. They might be working to change him 20% to 30% percent and think that this is acceptable if he loves her. However, basically men don't want to change for the love they already have. They want her to just accept that he is the way he is. They are willing to change a little just to try and make her happy. But it's the trying to change everything that a man will start to feel like she is not accepting him in the little things of life, then how is she going to accept the big things he does wrong?"

"So we might make him into a better dog or man only to lose him to someone else?"

"Yes, that is a possibility. We only want to train or change them, not break them."

"Well Julia...I have enjoyed our lunch today. I think maybe we should do this again next week. I am going to have to go home and think about all we discuss today. I am sure I will have some follow up questions for you."

"Yes, I would enjoy that... maybe we can talk more about the dogs .... and CATS!"

www.ingramcontent.com/pod-product-compliance
Lightning Source LLC
Chambersburg PA
CBHW071417040426
42445CB00012BA/1194